SPORTS SUPERSTARS

WHO IS CAITLIN CLARK?

PERCY LEED

Lerner Publications ◆ Minneapolis

Stats in this book are accurate through the 2024 Women's National Basketball Association season.

Lerner Publications Company
An imprint of Lerner Publishing Group, Inc.
241 First Avenue North
Minneapolis, MN 55401 USA

For reading levels and more information, look up this title at www.lernerbooks.com.

Main body text set in Mikado.
Typeface provided by HvD Fonts.

Designer: Mary Ross

Library of Congress Cataloging-in-Publication Data

Names: Leed, Percy, 1968- author
Title: Who is Caitlin Clark? : Indiana Fever superstar / Percy Leed.
Other titles: Indiana Fever superstar
Description: Minneapolis : Lerner Publications, [2026] | Series: Lerner sports rookie. Sports superstars | Includes bibliographical references and index. | Audience: Ages 5–8 | Audience: Grades 4–6 | Summary: "Indiana Fever star Caitlin Clark is the most popular player in women's basketball. Learn about her life and discover how she became college basketball's all-time leading scorer before taking the WNBA by storm"– Provided by publisher.
Identifiers: LCCN 2025015204 (print) | LCCN 2025015205 (ebook) | ISBN 9798765689592 library binding | ISBN 9798348029098 paperback | ISBN 9798765697788 epub
Subjects: LCSH: Clark, Caitlin, 2002- | Women basketball players—United States—Biography—Juvenile literature | Indiana Fever (Basketball team)—History—Juvenile literature
Classification: LCC GV884.C554 L44 2026 (print) | LCC GV884.C554 (ebook) | DDC 796.323092 [B]—dc23/eng/20250518

LC record available at https://lccn.loc.gov/2025015204
LC ebook record available at https://lccn.loc.gov/2025015205

Manufactured in the United States of America
1-1012368-54827-5/7/2025

TABLE OF CONTENTS

SHOOTING STAR

Caitlin Clark shot the basketball. She scored three points for the Indiana Fever!

Caitlin scored 35 points in the game. She set a new WNBA record!

Caitlin was born in Des Moines, Iowa, in 2002.

She loved to play sports. Her best sport was basketball.

In high school, Caitlin stood out. She was one of the best players in the United States.

Many college coaches wanted Caitlin to play for them. She chose the University of Iowa.

Caitlin was great in her first season. She led her team in scoring.

Caitlin got better every year.

In 2023, she led Iowa to the title game. Iowa lost to Louisiana State.

The next season was Caitlin's final season at Iowa. She became college basketball's all-time leading scorer!

Caitlin's success made her famous. Basketball fans everywhere cheered for her.

Caitlin led her team to the title game again. Iowa lost to South Carolina.

Caitlin's next stop was the WNBA. The Fever chose her with the first pick in the 2024 WNBA draft.

Her team did not play well at first. The Fever lost eight of their first nine games.

Caitlin and the team got better. They began to win more games.

Caitlin played hard. She was one of the best shooters in the WNBA. She made long shots that counted for three points.

Caitlin helped the Fever win 20 games in 2024. She won the WNBA Rookie of the Year award.

Caitlin wants to help girls become basketball stars like her. She also wants to win a WNBA title!

CAITLIN CLARK

2024 STATS

GAMES PLAYED:	40
POINTS:	769
THREE-POINT BASKETS:	122
ASSISTS:	337
STEALS:	53

CAITLIN CLARK
GEAR

GLOSSARY

draft: when teams take turns choosing new players

rookie: a first-year player

title: championship

WNBA: Women's National Basketball Association

LEARN MORE

Jeffries, Corina. *Caitlin Clark*. PowerKids, 2025.

Leed, Percy. *Basketball's NBA and WNBA Finals*. Lerner Publications, 2025.

Wagner, Zelda. *Basketball Superstars*. Lerner Publications, 2025.

INDEX

PHOTO ACKNOWLEDGMENTS

Chet White/Getty Images, pp. 5, 19; Monte Goodyk/Getty Images, p. 6; Marc Piscotty/Icon Sportswire via Getty Images, p. 7; AP Photo/Charlie Neibergall, p. 9; G Fiume/Maryland Terrapins/Getty Images, pp. 10, 23; Maddie Meyer/Getty Images, p. 12; Matthew Holst/Getty Images, p. 14; Dylan Buell/Getty Images, p. 17; David E. Klutho/Sports Illustrated via Getty Images, p. 21.
Cover: AP Photo/Michael Conroy.
Design elements: liangpv/Getty Images.